WELCOME TO UNITED STATES OF AMERICA

COUNTRIES OF THE WORLD

United States of America

by Kevin Kurtz

BLASTOFF! 2 READERS

BLASTOFF! READERS, AN IMPRINT OF BELLWETHER MEDIA BY FLUTTERBEE

Blastoff! Readers are carefully developed by literacy experts to build reading stamina and move students toward fluency by combining standards-based content with developmentally appropriate text.

LEVELS

Level 1 provides the most support through repetition of high-frequency words, light text, predictable sentence patterns, and strong visual support.

Level 2 offers early readers a bit more challenge through varied sentences, increased text load, and text-supportive special features.

Level 3 advances early-fluent readers toward fluency through increased text load, less reliance on photos, advancing concepts, longer sentences, and more complex special features.

★ **Blastoff! Universe**

Reading Level

Blastoff! Beginners — Grade K

Blastoff! Readers — Grades 1–3

Blastoff! Discovery — Grade 4

This edition first published in 2027 by Bellwether Media, Inc.

For information regarding permission, write to Bellwether Media, Inc., Attention: Permissions Department, 3500 American Blvd W, Suite 150, Bloomington, MN 55431.

Library of Congress Cataloging-in-Publication Data is available at www.loc.gov or upon request from the publisher.

ISBN: 9798898800505 (hardcover)
ISBN: 9798898801748 (ebook)

Editor: Betsy Rathburn Designer: Laura Sowers

Printed in the United States of America, North Mankato, MN.

Table of Contents

All About the United States of America

Washington, DC

The United States of America is a large country in North America. Its capital is Washington, DC.

American movies and music are popular around the world.

Land and Animals

The Mississippi River flows through many states. The **Great Plains** are covered in grass.

The Atlantic, Pacific, and Arctic Oceans touch the coasts. Western mountains rise high.

Great Plains

Yellowstone National Park

Size: around 3,472 square miles (8,992 square kilometers)

Famous For: became the first national park and has many water features

The Southeast is hot and **humid**. The north is cooler. Little rain falls in the Southwest.

Northern Alaska is in the **Arctic Circle**. Winters are cold and dark. Hawaii is **tropical**.

Bald eagles dive for fish in lakes. Horseshoe crabs lay eggs on East Coast beaches.

Animals of the United States of America

bald eagle

Atlantic horseshoe crab

American bison

western diamondback rattlesnake

Bison eat **prairie** grass. **Desert** rattlesnakes warn **predators** to stay away.

Life in the United States of America

Americans have **ancestors** from around the world. The main language is English.

Most Americans live in cities. Most people are **Christians**.

Many Americans play video games. Football is the most popular sport.

People enjoy visiting parks.
They hike, fish, and camp.

Many Americans enjoy hamburgers. S'mores and chocolate chip cookies are popular sweets.

American Foods

hamburgers

s'mores

tacos

pizza

Foods from other countries are popular. Tacos are from Mexico. Pizza is from Italy.

Independence Day is a summer holiday. People have cookouts and watch fireworks.

Thanksgiving is in November. People gather to eat a big meal. Americans love to **celebrate**!

Thanksgiving

Independence Day

United States of America Facts

Size:
3,796,742 square miles
(9,833,517 square kilometers)

Population:
340,587,000 (2026)

National Holiday:
Independence Day (July 4)

Main Language:
English

Capital City:
Washington, DC

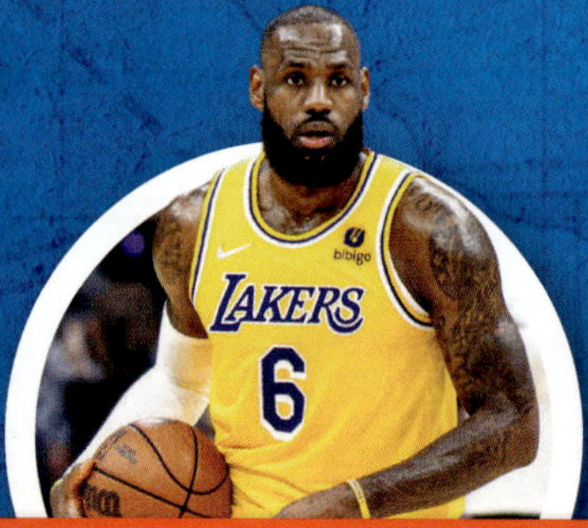

Famous Face

Name: LeBron James
Famous For: one of the greatest basketball players of all time

Religions

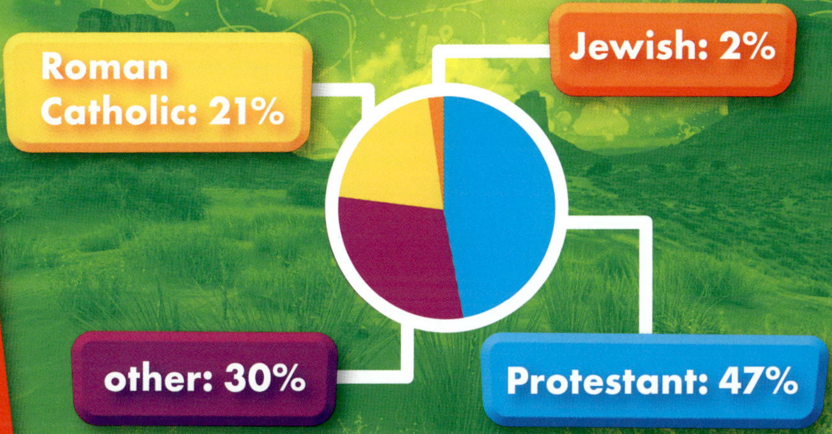

Top Landmarks

Golden Gate Bridge

Grand Canyon

Statue of Liberty

Glossary

ancestors—relatives who lived long ago

Arctic Circle—an imaginary line that circles the top of the globe, parallel to the equator

celebrate—to do something special or fun for an event, occasion, or holiday

Christians—people who believe in the words of Jesus Christ

desert—related to areas that have dry land with few plants and little rainfall

Great Plains—a region of flat or gently rolling land in the central United States

humid—having a lot of water in the air

independence—related to freedom from being under control of someone or something

prairie—related to large grasslands that are mostly flat and treeless

predators—animals that hunt other animals for food

tropical—having to do with a place that is hot and wet

To Learn More

AT THE LIBRARY

Downs, Kieran. *LeBron James.* Minneapolis, Minn.: Bellwether Media, 2023.

Fabiny, Sarah. *Where Is Yellowstone?* New York, N.Y.: Penguin Workshop, 2024.

National Geographic Society. *Kids Beginner's United States Atlas.* Washington, D.C.: National Geographic Kids, 2023.

ON THE WEB

FACTSURFER

Factsurfer.com gives you a safe, fun way to find more information.

1. Go to www.factsurfer.com.
2. Enter "United States of America" into the search box and click 🔍.
3. Select your book cover to see a list of related content.

Index

The images in this book are reproduced through the courtesy of: THANANIT, front cover; SeanPavonePhoto, front cover; Rawpixel.com, p. 3; lunamarina, pp. 4-5; Andrew, p. 6; Daphne, pp. 6-7; winterbilder, pp. 8-9; blvdone, p. 9; Gabi Luka, pp. 10-11; Gregory Johnston, p. 11 (bald eagle); SailingAway, p. 11 (Atlantic horseshoe crab); Jillian, p. 11 (American bison); Tom, p. 11 (western diamondback rattlesnake); Brian, p. 12; Chalermphon, pp. 12-13; Tinxi, p. 14; Ringo Chiu, pp. 14-15; Billy McDonald, p. 15; koss13, p. 16 (hamburgers); Brent Hofacker, p. 16 (s'mores, tacos); fudio, p. 16 (pizza); Anastasia Stygailo, p. 17; Monkey Business, p. 18; ALFSnaiper, pp. 18-19; somartin, p. 20 (flag); Erik Drost/ Wikipedia, p. 20 (LeBron James); Martin M303, p. 21 (Golden Gate Bridge); Sumiko Scott, p. 21 (Grand Canyon); mshch, p. 21 (Statue of Liberty); Hanoi.s, p. 22.